My Super Activity Book

LINES & SHAPES
PENCIL FUN

This Book Belongs To

_____

Yummy in my Tummy

Help these cute animals reach their favourite food by joining the dotted lines!

Wavy Lines

Trace the dotted lines from left to right and complete the sea waves!

Home, Sweet Home

Help Manny reach his house after a long day at school by tracing the path.

Chef's Magic

Complete the spirals to taste chef Charlie's delicious dishes!

Playful Squirrel

Help the squirrel cross the maze to reach the peanuts.

Radiant Rainbow

Trace the dotted lines and colour the illustration to match the coloured image.

Zigzag Lines

Trace the zigzag patterns for the water drops to fall into the buckets.

Curves

Connect the roads and the vehicles by tracing the dotted red lines.

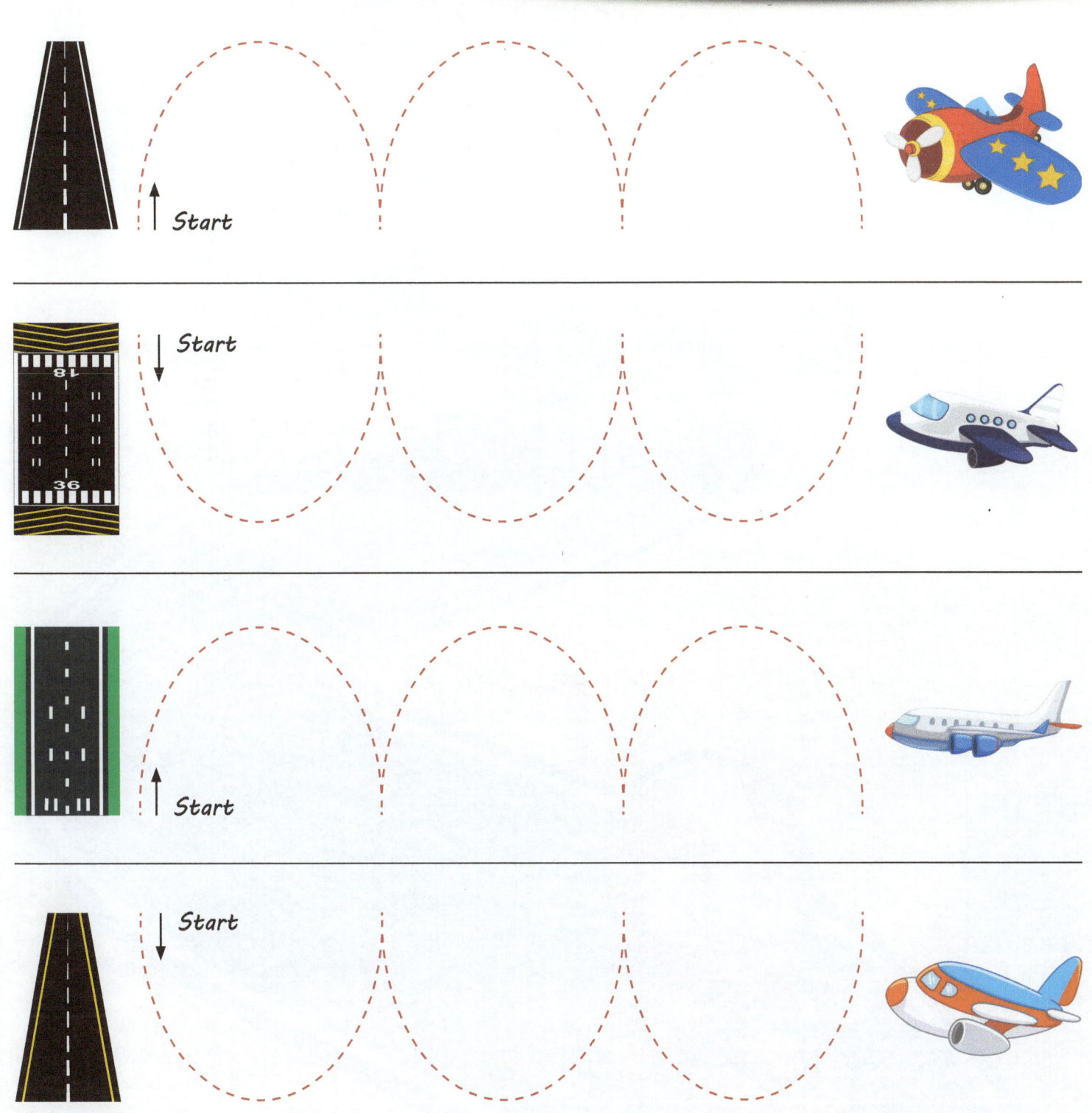

Go-Karting Mania

Trace the dotted lines to complete the go-karting track.

Tilted Lines

Complete the slanting patterns by joining the dotted lines!

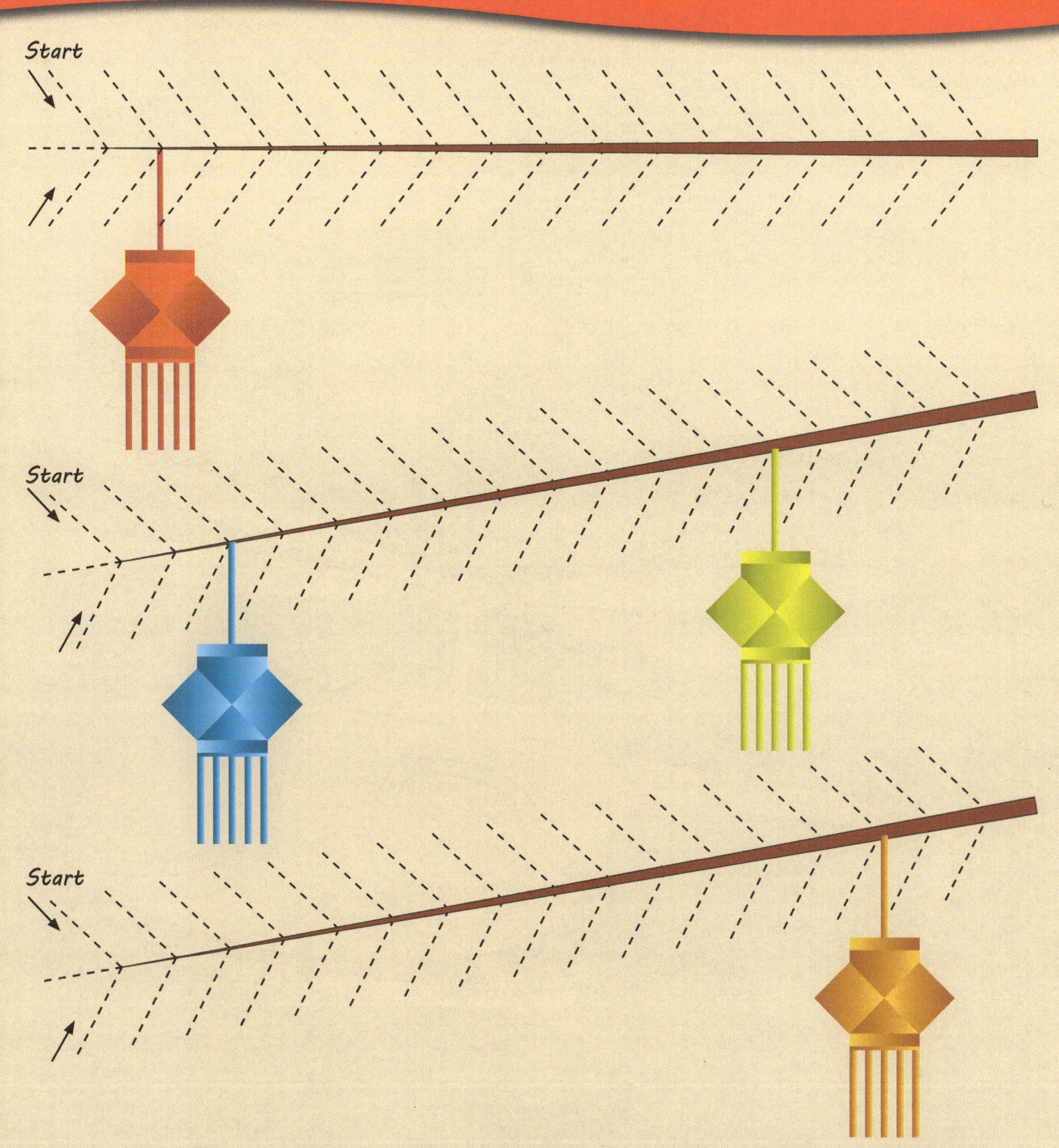

Fly High!

Trace the dotted lines to make the helicopter fly high in the sky. Next, colour it.

Wavy Patterns

Trace the dotted lines and connect the balloons to the pencils.

Tasty Treats

Complete these lip-smacking combos by joining the dotted lines!

Colourful Candy

Trace the spirals to complete the sweet lollipops!

Little Birdie
Join the dotted lines to complete the little bird. Next, colour her.

Sunny Summer

Complete the sun's rays by tracing the dotted lines.

Lines and Vehicles

Trace the lines and match the twin vehicles.

My Home

Trace the dotted lines from the 'Start' point to complete the house. Next, colour it.

Spiral Patterns

Trace the lines and complete the snakes' bodies.

Bubbly Bees

Trace the lines to help the bees reach the flowers!

Start

Start

Start

Start

Start

Sparkly Seashells

Complete the seashells on the sea shore!

Starry Night

Join the dots and complete the shining stars!

Juicy Grapes

Trace the dotted patterns to complete the juicy green grapes.

Dainty Deer

Trace the dotted lines to complete the deer.
Next, fill colours in them.

Flower Shower

Trace the dotted lines to complete the colourful flowers.

Jungle Joy

Trace the red dotted lines to reach the fallen fruits.

Bella, The Butterfly

Trace lines from numbers 1-20, to complete beautiful Bella. Next, colour her.

Cheesy Pizza

Trace the dotted lines to complete the cheesy pizza.

Spooky Halloween

Trace the shapes within the Halloween pumpkins.

Creamy Chocolate

Trace the straight lines to complete the creamy chocolate bar. Next, colour it brown.

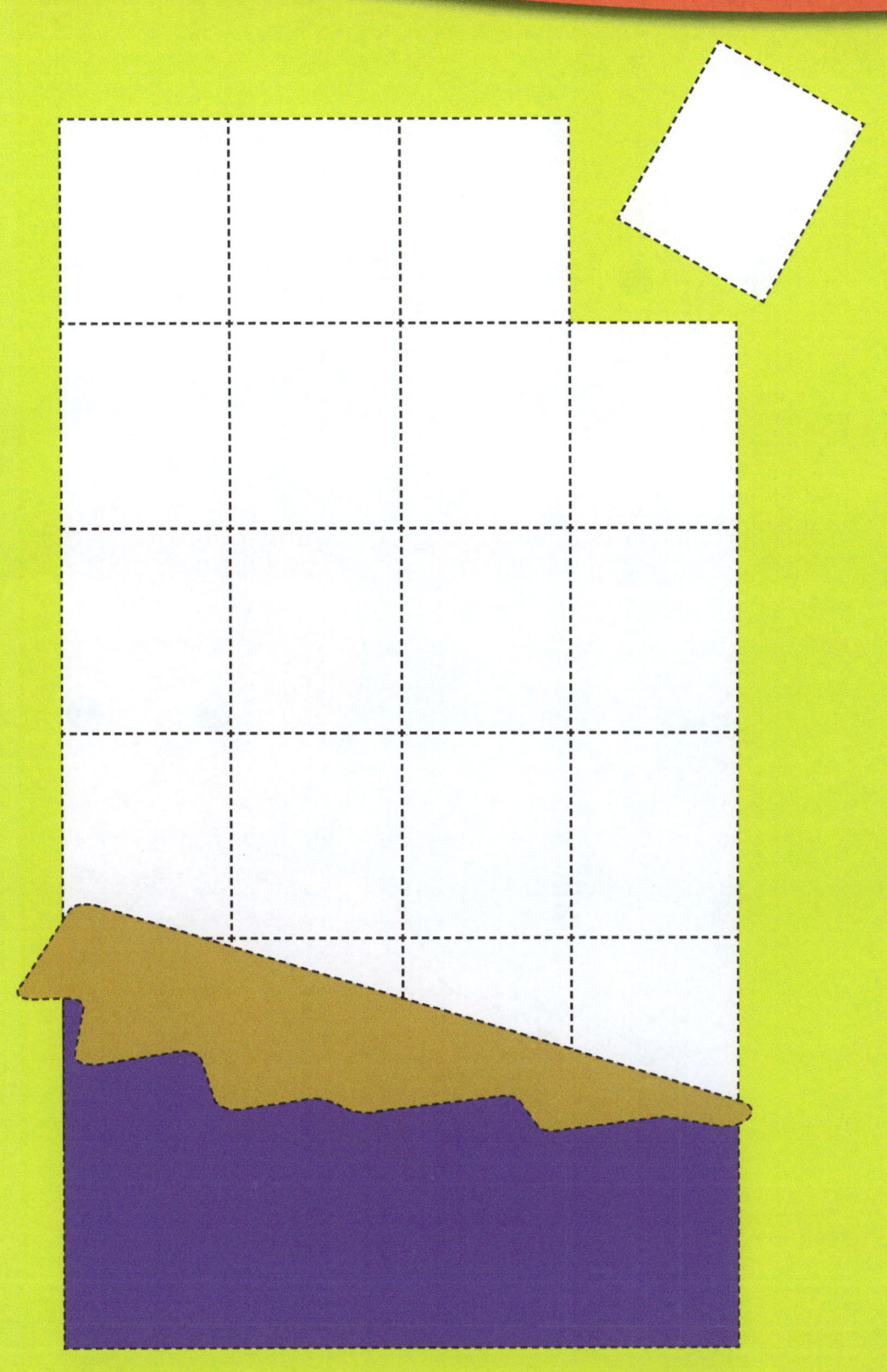

Awesome Octopuses

Join the dots to complete the pink octopuses.

Merry Christmas!

Trace the dotted lines to complete Santa's stocking.

Jimmy & Timmy

Trace the path so that Jimmy can reach Timmy!

Smoky Spirals

Complete the smoky spirals below.

Bob, the Baby Elephant

Help Bob take a bath by joining the dotted lines!

Jolly Journey

Help the persons reach the vehicles to begin their journey, by joining the two pink dots.

Taxi Driver

Taxi

Pilot

Aeroplane

Captain

Ship

Sweet and Sour Noodles

Trace the wavy lines to enjoy the delicious noodles.

Happy Birthday!

Trace the dotted lines and colour the candles to complete the cake.

Magical Butterflies

Trace the dotted lines to complete the butterflies. Colour them next.

Steve, The Snowman

Join the dotted lines to complete Steve.

Lighthouse

Trace the lines to spread the beams of the lighthouse.

Emergency Helpers

Help the emergency helpers reach their vehicles.

Delicious Ice Cream

Trace the dotted lines to complete the image below.

Rainbow Umbrella

Connect the white dots to complete the rainbow-coloured umbrella.

A Winding Maze

Trace the path to help the red car reach home!

Rising Rocket

Help the rocket soar high into space by joining the dotted lines.

Glowing Bulbs

Complete the glowing bulbs by joining the dotted lines. Next, colour them.